Understanding and Celebrating Autism : A Beginner's Comprehensive Guide

Nedia Mandhouj

Published by Nedia Mandhouj, 2023.

UNDERSTANDING AND CELEBRATING AUTISM : A BEGINNER'S COMPREHENSIVE GUIDE

First edition. December 3, 2023.

Copyright © 2023 Nedia Mandhouj.

ISBN: 979-8223932154

Written by Nedia Mandhouj.

Also by Nedia Mandhouj

Understanding and Celebrating Autism : A Beginner's Comprehensive Guide

Table of Contents

Table of content

Conclusion

A. Recap of Key Points
B. Encouragement for individuals with autism and their families

Introduction

Welcome Note

Dear Reader,

Welcome to "Understanding Autism: A Compassionate Guide." Your decision to explore this book marks a significant step toward embracing empathy, fostering understanding, and celebrating the vibrant spectrum of autism.

In these pages, we embark on a journey—a journey of discovery, appreciation, and acceptance. Autism, with its unique colors and diverse experiences, invites us to view the world through different lenses, embracing the beauty of neurodiversity.

This book isn't just a collection of words; it's an invitation to delve into the rich tapestry of the human mind and heart. Through shared stories, insights, and knowledge, we aim to foster a community of understanding and support.

Whether you're a parent seeking guidance, an educator expanding your knowledge, or someone eager to learn more about autism, I invite you to engage, explore, and embrace the stories waiting within these chapters.

Let us embark on this journey with open hearts and open minds. Together, let's celebrate the uniqueness, acknowledge the strengths, and build a world that honors and embraces the diversity of every individual.

Thank you for choosing to understand autism. Your commitment to learning is a beacon of hope for a more inclusive and compassionate world.

Warm regards,
Mandhouj Nadiya

Why Understanding Autism is Important

Autism is a part of the diversity in our world. Just like people have different interests, talents, and ways of thinking, autism reflects a unique way of experiencing the world. Understanding autism is crucial because it helps us create a more inclusive and supportive society for everyone.

Firstly, when we understand autism, we learn to appreciate diversity better. It's about recognizing that everyone has their strengths and challenges. Autism is no different – it's a different way of thinking, not a limitation. Embracing this diversity enriches our communities and encourages acceptance.

Secondly, understanding autism promotes empathy and kindness. When we learn about the experiences of individuals on the autism spectrum, it helps us put ourselves in their shoes. This empathy leads to better interactions, fostering a culture of understanding and support.

Moreover, learning about autism is practical. It equips us with knowledge to provide appropriate support. Whether in schools, workplaces, or communities, this understanding helps create environments where everyone can thrive. Teachers, employers, and families can adapt and provide better assistance when needed.

Another significant aspect is breaking stereotypes and misconceptions. Misunderstandings about autism can lead to unfair judgments and exclusion. By learning about autism, we challenge these misconceptions and foster a more inclusive environment where everyone feels respected and valued.

Ultimately, understanding autism is about creating a world where differences are not only accepted but celebrated. It's about building communities where everyone has the opportunity to contribute and be appreciated for their unique perspectives.

Chapter 1: What is Autism Spectrum Disorder?

In this chapter, we delve into Autism Spectrum Disorder (ASD) with brevity and depth, offering a succinct yet comprehensive understanding. We begin by defining autism, unraveling its fundamental traits that shape how individuals perceive and interact with the world. Moving through the historical narrative, we trace the evolution of our comprehension of autism, exploring pivotal moments that have shaped our understanding. Lastly, we debunk prevalent misconceptions and myths surrounding ASD, aiming to provide clarity and empathy in understanding individuals on the autism spectrum. Through these subchapters, our aim is to offer a concise exploration that sheds light on the diverse and intricate nature of Autism Spectrum Disorder.

Defining Autism

Autism Spectrum Disorder (ASD) represents a complex neurodevelopmental condition that profoundly influences how individuals perceive and engage with the world. This condition encompasses a broad spectrum, showcasing a diverse range of strengths, challenges, and unique characteristics among those affected. Imagine this spectrum as a multifaceted tapestry, where each individual embodies a distinctive thread, displaying varying colors and patterns of abilities and difficulties. Within this spectrum, individuals may excel in specific areas such as art, music, mathematics, or memory, while grappling with challenges in social interactions, communication nuances, or adapting to changes in routine or environment. The defining traits at the core of autism often involve difficulties in social interaction and communication, manifesting as challenges in understanding emotions, maintaining eye contact, interpreting social cues, and engaging in reciprocal conversations. Repetitive behaviors, adherence to routines, and intense focus on specific topics or activities are commonly observed traits. Early signs of autism might emerge in early childhood, ranging from delayed speech or language development to repetitive movements or fixations on particular objects or subjects. Diagnosis involves a comprehensive evaluation by healthcare professionals skilled in assessing behavior, communication patterns, and social interactions. Over time, perceptions of autism have evolved, transitioning from a poorly understood or rare condition to a recognized spectrum characterized by diversity. The emergence of the neurodiversity movement advocates for celebrating the unique strengths and perspectives individuals with autism bring to society, promoting inclusivity and acceptance. Living with autism can present challenges, necessitating tailored support strategies in education, employment, and social integration. Therapies, interventions, and accommodations aim to nurture strengths and assist individuals in overcoming obstacles, thereby fostering a more inclusive and understanding environment. Understanding autism involves recognizing its spectrum nature, acknowledging its core characteristics, identifying early signs, embracing diverse perspectives, and providing tailored support for individuals across the spectrum.

History and Evolution of Understanding Autism

The history of autism traces back through time, but people didn't understand it until more recently. In ancient times, stories sometimes mentioned behaviors that remind us of autism, but they were seen differently back then. During the Middle Ages and the Renaissance, some people noticed behaviors similar to autism, but they didn't recognize it as a specific condition.

It wasn't until the 20th century that doctors started to study autism more seriously. In 1943, two doctors, Leo Kanner and Hans Asperger, separately wrote about children who had trouble communicating and acting differently. Kanner called it 'early infantile autism', and Asperger talked about 'Asperger's syndrome'. These studies were essential because they helped people understand that autism was a real thing, but the understanding was limited at first.

As time passed, doctors learned more about autism and how it affects people differently. They started to include many different behaviors and symptoms under the term 'Autism Spectrum Disorder' (ASD). This meant that autism wasn't just one thing; it was a spectrum, like a big rainbow with many colors.

Over the years, people's ideas about autism have changed. Instead of only seeing it as something bad or different, some people now see it as part of the wonderful diversity in the world. They say 'neurodiversity' to mean that everyone's brain works in its unique way, and that's okay.

Scientists have also been studying autism a lot. They look at how our genes and brains might be connected to autism. They want to understand it better so they can help people who have autism.

Understanding autism has been a journey with many changes. We have learned a lot, but there's still more to discover. The important thing is to keep learning, supporting each other, and treating everyone with kindness and understanding.

Misconceptions and Myths

Understanding autism involves debunking various misconceptions and myths that have circulated about this complex condition. Misconceptions often stem from limited awareness, stereotypes, and misinformation. Let's delve into and dispel some of the most common misconceptions and myths surrounding autism:

- **<u>Autism is Caused by Bad Parenting or Vaccines:</u>** One of the most persistent myths is that negligent parenting or childhood vaccines cause autism. However, extensive research by medical professionals and scientific studies has disproven these claims. Autism is a complex neurodevelopmental condition influenced by genetic and environmental factors, not by parenting practices or vaccines.

- **<u>People with Autism Lack Empathy:</u>** Contrary to the belief that individuals with autism lack empathy, many actually feel empathy deeply. However, they might express it differently or struggle to interpret social cues, which can give the impression of a lack of empathy. In reality, people with autism can be highly empathetic, but their way of showing it might be unique.

- **<u>All Individuals with Autism Have Exceptional Savant Skills:</u>** While some individuals with autism possess extraordinary talents or skills in specific areas, such as music, art, or mathematics, it's not a universal characteristic. Only a small percentage of people with autism exhibit savant abilities. Autism manifests differently in each person, and not everyone has exceptional skills.

- **<u>People with Autism Are Violent or Aggressive:</u>** This misconception is false and harmful. Individuals with autism are not inherently violent or aggressive. However, they may experience sensory overload or difficulties in communicating their needs, which can lead to frustration or meltdowns. With understanding and appropriate support, these instances can be minimized.

- **<u>Autism Only Affects Children:</u>** Autism is a lifelong condition that affects individuals across their lifespan. While early intervention is crucial for children with autism, adults also live with and manage the challenges and strengths associated with autism. Understanding and support are essential for individuals of all ages on the autism spectrum.

- **<u>Individuals with Autism Lack Intelligence:</u>** Intelligence is diverse among individuals with autism. While some may have intellectual disabilities, others have average or above-average intelligence. Intelligence and autism are not mutually exclusive, and many individuals with autism have unique strengths and abilities.

Dispelling myths and misconceptions is crucial to fostering a more informed and inclusive society. Understanding that autism is a diverse spectrum and challenging false beliefs can create a more accepting and supportive environment for individuals with autism.

Chapter 2: Understanding the Autism Spectrum

The autism spectrum is a diverse landscape encompassing a wide array of individual differences and unique traits. This chapter delves into the multifaceted nature of the spectrum, exploring its diversity, the varying degrees of support individuals might require, and the defining characteristics that contribute to the understanding of autism. It discusses the varied strengths, challenges, and individual nuances present within the spectrum, the spectrum's diverse support needs, and an overview of the distinct traits associated with autism, such as social communication differences, sensory sensitivities, repetitive behaviors, and distinct interests.

Spectrum Diversity and Individual Differences

Understanding autism as a spectrum involves acknowledging the vast array of diversities and unique traits present within it. The autism spectrum is not a one-size-fits-all category but rather a spectrum that encompasses an extensive range of characteristics, abilities, and challenges.

Understanding the Spectrum

At its core, the spectrum acknowledges that each person with autism is unique. The diversity within the spectrum means that individuals may experience autism differently, presenting an incredible variety of strengths and areas of difficulty. While some may excel in specific skills like mathematics, art, or music, others may face challenges in social interactions or sensory processing. This diversity highlights the richness and complexity of the autistic community.

Individual Differences

Individual differences are key components of the spectrum. No two individuals with autism are alike, emphasizing the importance of recognizing and celebrating these differences. Some individuals might prefer routines and predictability, finding comfort in structured environments, while others might exhibit a range of preferences and behaviors. Understanding these individual differences fosters a more inclusive and accommodating environment that respects the diverse needs of individuals across the spectrum.

Embracing Neurodiversity

Embracing neurodiversity involves acknowledging that differences in brain function and behavior are a natural part of human diversity. It encourages a shift away from viewing autism as solely a disorder but rather as a different way of experiencing the world. This perspective celebrates the unique talents and perspectives that individuals with autism bring to society, emphasizing the value of their contributions.

The Importance of Acceptance

Recognizing and embracing the diverse nature of the autism spectrum is crucial in creating an inclusive and supportive society. Acceptance encourages an environment where individuals feel understood, respected, and accommodated based on their specific needs and strengths. By fostering acceptance and understanding, we can build a world that values and celebrates diversity in all its forms.

Levels of Support Needed

Understanding the varying levels of support required by individuals within the autism spectrum is crucial in providing appropriate care and fostering inclusivity.

The spectrum of autism encompasses a wide range of support needs, from minimal assistance to extensive support across different aspects of life. It's essential to recognize that each person's requirements for support are unique, influenced by factors such as communication skills, sensory sensitivities, and social interactions.

Levels of Support

Support needs can vary significantly among individuals with autism. Some individuals may require minimal support, perhaps in specific areas such as organizing tasks or managing sensory inputs. Others might need moderate support, including guidance in social situations or developing strategies to cope with sensory sensitivities. Additionally, some individuals might require significant support in most aspects of daily life, including communication, daily routines, and social interactions.

Tailoring Support

Tailoring support to meet individual needs is critical. Approaches and interventions should be personalized, focusing on strengths while addressing areas that require support. Creating individualized plans that consider the person's preferences, abilities, and challenges is fundamental in providing effective support.

Factors Influencing Support

Several factors influence the level of support an individual with autism may require. These include their age, developmental stage, co-occurring conditions (such as ADHD or anxiety), and access to resources and services. Understanding these factors helps in creating comprehensive support plans that cater to specific needs.

Building Support Networks

Constructing robust support networks involving family, educators, therapists, and community resources is vital. Collaborating with these networks ensures a holistic approach to support, allowing for consistency and continuity in care across different environments.

Empowerment and Autonomy

Encouraging autonomy and empowering individuals with autism to make choices and participate actively in their support plans is essential. Respecting their preferences and involving them in decision-making processes promotes a sense of ownership and self-determination.

Recognizing the diverse support needs within the autism spectrum is pivotal in creating an inclusive and supportive environment. By acknowledging individual differences and tailoring support accordingly, we can ensure that everyone receives the necessary assistance to thrive and participate fully in society.

Characteristics of Autism

Understanding the fundamental characteristics of autism is essential to grasp the broad spectrum of behaviors and traits encompassed by this condition.

Autism Spectrum Disorder (ASD) manifests in a wide array of characteristics that significantly impact an individual's social interactions, communication, behavior, and sensory experiences. These characteristics are unique to each person on the spectrum and present themselves in various ways, ranging from mild to severe.

Individuals with autism often experience difficulties in social interaction and communication. Challenges may include difficulty in understanding social cues, maintaining eye contact, interpreting facial expressions, or engaging in reciprocal conversations. Social situations might be overwhelming, leading to social anxiety or difficulty in forming relationships.

Communication difficulties can range from delayed language development to atypical speech patterns or a preference for non-verbal communication. Some individuals might have a vast vocabulary but struggle with pragmatic language, such as understanding idioms or sarcasm. Others may use echolalia or repetitive language.

A common characteristic includes engaging in repetitive behaviors or exhibiting specific, focused interests. These behaviors might involve repetitive movements (stimming), adherence to rigid routines, or a fixation on specific topics or objects. The intensity and nature of these interests can vary widely among individuals.

Many individuals with autism experience sensory sensitivities. They may be hypersensitive or hyposensitive to sensory stimuli, such as touch, sound, taste, smell, or visual input. Sensory overload or discomfort in certain environments can trigger distress or emotional reactions.

While challenges are evident, individuals with autism also possess unique strengths. Some exhibit remarkable attention to detail, exceptional memory, creativity, and specialized skills in areas such as mathematics, music, or art.

Understanding the characteristics of autism involves recognizing the multifaceted nature of its traits, which vary widely among individuals. Embracing these differences and acknowledging the strengths within the spectrum promotes inclusivity and supports the development of tailored interventions and support systems for individuals with autism.

Chapter 3: Signs and Symptoms of Autism

Chapter 3 is a comprehensive exploration into the telltale signs and distinct characteristics that define autism. This chapter navigates through the intricate landscape of autism spectrum disorder, beginning with A. Early Signs in Infants and Toddlers, shedding light on the subtle cues that might signal autism's presence in the earliest stages of life. It progresses into B. Common Behaviors and Traits, unveiling a spectrum of behaviors observed across various age groups. Lastly, the chapter delves into C. Co-occurring Conditions and Comorbidities, highlighting additional conditions often associated with autism, offering a holistic understanding of its complexities.

Early Signs in Infants and Toddlers

Understanding the early signs of autism in infants and toddlers is crucial for early identification and intervention. While every child develops differently, some early indicators might suggest the possibility of autism spectrum disorder (ASD). It's important to note that these signs don't necessarily confirm autism but can prompt further evaluation by healthcare professionals.

Delayed Developmental Milestones:

Infants and toddlers usually reach developmental milestones in areas like speech, social interaction, and motor skills at predictable ages. Delayed achievement of these milestones might indicate a potential concern. For instance, not responding to their name by 12 months, lack of babbling or pointing by 12 months, or not using single words by 16-18 months could raise red flags.

Limited Eye Contact and Social Interaction:

Many children with autism tend to avoid eye contact or display challenges in engaging socially. Infants and toddlers might show less interest in making eye contact, avoiding reciprocal smiles or interactions, or seem disinterested in social games like peek-a-boo or pat-a-cake.

Repetitive Behaviors and Sensory Sensitivities:

Some infants and toddlers with autism might display repetitive behaviors, like hand flapping, rocking, or fixation on specific objects. Sensory sensitivities, such as being overly sensitive or under-responsive to certain sounds, textures, or lights, can also be observed.

Communication Difficulties:

Challenges in communication can manifest early. Infants might not respond to their name being called or show less interest in imitation or simple gestures like waving or pointing. Limited attempts at vocalizations, lack of babbling or using gestures by 12 months, and delayed speech development are signs to be mindful of.

Preference for Routine and Resistance to Change:

Some infants and toddlers with autism might display an extreme liking for routine and become distressed with changes. They might prefer repetitive play activities or show resistance when a change occurs in their environment or daily routine.

Unusual Interests or Intense Focus:

Children with autism might exhibit intense interests in certain objects or activities. They might focus extensively on a single object or topic, displaying intense fascination that seems beyond typical developmental exploration.

Understanding and recognizing these early signs can be beneficial in seeking early intervention and support for children who may require additional evaluation and assistance in their development. However, it's crucial to consult healthcare professionals for proper evaluation and guidance if any concerns arise.

Common Behaviors and Traits

Understanding common behaviors and traits associated with autism is essential in comprehending the spectrum of this neurological condition. While behaviors and characteristics may vary significantly among individuals, certain patterns are frequently observed.

Repetitive Behaviors:

Individuals with autism often engage in repetitive behaviors, such as hand flapping, body rocking, or repeating phrases or actions. These actions provide comfort or help in managing sensory overload.

Sensory Sensitivities:

Many autistic individuals experience heightened or reduced sensitivity to sensory stimuli, such as sound, touch, taste, or smell. For instance, they might be overwhelmed by loud noises or specific textures.

Difficulty in Social Interactions:

Challenges in social interactions are common among individuals with autism. They may struggle with understanding social cues, maintaining eye contact, or interpreting facial expressions and emotions.

Special Interests and Routines:

Individuals with autism often exhibit intense interests in specific subjects or activities. They may adhere rigidly to routines and become distressed if there are changes or disruptions.

Communication Differences:

Verbal and non-verbal communication differences are prevalent in autism. Some may have delayed speech development, use echolalia (repeating words or phrases), or have difficulty initiating or sustaining conversations.

Emotional Regulation Challenges:

Managing emotions can be challenging for individuals with autism. They may have difficulty expressing emotions or understanding others' feelings, leading to outbursts or meltdowns.

Strengths and Unique Abilities:

While focusing on challenges, it's important to highlight the strengths and unique abilities of individuals with autism. Many have exceptional memory, attention to detail, creativity, or proficiency in specific areas of interest.

Understanding these common behaviors and traits can foster greater empathy and support for individuals with autism. Embracing neurodiversity and appreciating the unique perspectives and abilities of those on the spectrum can promote inclusivity and acceptance in society.

Co-occurring Conditions and Comorbidities

Understanding the various co-occurring conditions and comorbidities that often accompany autism spectrum disorder (ASD) is crucial to gain a comprehensive perspective on the complexities of this neurodevelopmental condition. Individuals with autism commonly experience a range of additional conditions that can impact their overall well-being and require specialized attention and care.

Intellectual Disabilities:

A significant proportion of individuals with autism exhibit varying degrees of intellectual disabilities, affecting cognitive abilities such as reasoning, problem-solving, and adaptive functioning. These challenges can impact learning and daily living skills.

Attention-Deficit/Hyperactivity Disorder (ADHD):

ADHD frequently co-occurs with autism. Symptoms like impulsivity, hyperactivity, and difficulties in sustaining attention can exacerbate social and behavioral challenges in individuals with autism.

Anxiety Disorders:

Anxiety disorders, including generalized anxiety, social anxiety, or specific phobias, are commonly observed in individuals on the autism spectrum. These conditions can heighten stress levels, impacting social interactions and daily functioning.

Depression and Mood Disorders:

Depression and mood disorders are prevalent among individuals with autism. Challenges related to social communication, sensory sensitivities, and difficulties in understanding social cues can contribute to these conditions.

Epilepsy and Seizure Disorders:

There's an increased prevalence of epilepsy and seizure disorders among individuals with autism. Managing these conditions alongside the core symptoms of autism requires specialized care and attention.

Gastrointestinal (GI) Issues:

Gastrointestinal problems such as irritable bowel syndrome (IBS), constipation, or gastroesophageal reflux disease (GERD) are frequently reported in individuals with autism. These issues can affect overall comfort and well-being.

Sensory Processing Disorders (SPD):

Many individuals with autism experience challenges with sensory processing, resulting in heightened sensitivities or difficulties in regulating sensory input. These sensory issues can significantly impact daily life.

Sleep Disorders:

Sleep disturbances are common in individuals with autism. Irregular sleep patterns, insomnia, or difficulties in falling and staying asleep can affect overall health and daily functioning.

Understanding and addressing these co-occurring conditions and comorbidities are crucial for providing comprehensive care and support to individuals with autism. Tailoring interventions and therapies to address these additional challenges is essential in improving their overall quality of life and well-being.

Chapter 4: Diagnosis and Evaluation

This chapter delves into the critical aspects of diagnosing and assessing Autism Spectrum Disorder (ASD). It explores the diagnostic process, the roles of various professionals involved, and the assessments and criteria used to determine an ASD diagnosis. Understanding how diagnoses are made, the specialists involved, and the evaluation methods employed provides essential insights into recognizing and confirming autism, aiding families and individuals in accessing appropriate support and interventions.

The Diagnostic Process

The process of diagnosing Autism Spectrum Disorder (ASD) involves a comprehensive evaluation to identify and understand the distinctive behavioral patterns and social communication difficulties that characterize this neurodevelopmental condition. Understanding the steps involved in the diagnostic journey provides a foundational insight into recognizing and confirming ASD.

- **Recognizing Early Signs:**

The diagnostic process often begins with the recognition of early signs or atypical behaviors observed in children during their developmental stages. These signs may include challenges in social interaction, delayed language development, repetitive behaviors, and sensory sensitivities. It's crucial for parents, caregivers, and healthcare professionals to recognize these indicators early on to initiate timely assessments.

- **Seeking Professional Evaluation:**

Upon recognizing potential signs of ASD, seeking a professional evaluation becomes pivotal. This typically involves consulting pediatricians, child psychologists, developmental pediatricians, or specialized clinicians trained in assessing neurodevelopmental disorders. These professionals conduct a series of evaluations, considering various aspects of a child's development and behavior.

- **Comprehensive Assessment and Observation:**

A thorough assessment is conducted, involving observations, interviews, and standardized tests tailored to evaluate social communication, language skills, behavioral patterns, and cognitive abilities. These assessments may include the Autism Diagnostic Observation Schedule (ADOS) and Autism Diagnostic Interview-Revised (ADI-R), among others, to gather comprehensive information.

- **Collaboration and Information Gathering:**

The diagnostic process often involves collaboration among multidisciplinary teams, including psychologists, speech-language therapists, occupational therapists, and educators. Gathering information from multiple sources, such as parents, teachers, and caregivers, contributes to a holistic understanding of the individual's behavior and development.

- **Evaluation of Diagnostic Criteria:**

Clinicians assess the individual's symptoms against the diagnostic criteria outlined in standard classification systems, such as the DSM-5 (Diagnostic and Statistical Manual of Mental Disorders) or ICD-10 (International Classification of Diseases). Meeting specific criteria is crucial to establishing a formal diagnosis of ASD.

- **Differential Diagnosis and Ruling Out Other Conditions:**

Clinicians also consider other developmental disorders and medical conditions that might mimic ASD symptoms. Ruling out conditions like intellectual disabilities, language disorders, or social anxiety is important to ensure an accurate diagnosis.

- **Provision of Feedback and Guidance:**

After the evaluation process, clinicians provide feedback to parents or guardians, explaining the assessment results and the subsequent diagnosis. They offer guidance on available interventions, therapies, and support services tailored to the individual's needs.

Understanding the diagnostic process offers a foundational understanding of the journey individuals and families undertake in confirming and understanding Autism Spectrum Disorder. It underscores the significance of early recognition, comprehensive evaluation, and collaborative efforts among professionals to provide timely interventions and support.

Types of Professionals Involved

The journey towards understanding and supporting individuals with Autism Spectrum Disorder (ASD) involves a collaborative effort from various professionals spanning different disciplines. Understanding the roles and contributions of these professionals is crucial in providing comprehensive care and support for individuals on the spectrum.

– Pediatricians and General Practitioners:

Pediatricians or general practitioners are often the initial point of contact for parents seeking guidance on their child's developmental concerns. They play a pivotal role in identifying developmental delays and referring families to specialists for further assessment and evaluation.

– Child Psychologists and Psychiatrists:

Child psychologists and psychiatrists specialize in assessing behavioral and mental health concerns in children and adolescents. They conduct comprehensive evaluations to diagnose ASD, provide therapy, and offer guidance for managing behavioral challenges.

– Developmental Pediatricians and Neurologists:

Developmental pediatricians and neurologists have expertise in neurodevelopmental disorders. They assess and diagnose ASD, addressing the developmental aspects and potential neurological underpinnings associated with the condition.

– Speech-Language Pathologists (SLPs):

SLPs evaluate and address communication challenges in individuals with ASD. They help improve speech, language, and social communication skills, offering interventions tailored to the specific needs of each individual.

– Occupational Therapists (OTs):

OTs focus on enhancing fine motor skills, sensory processing, and adaptive behaviors. They provide strategies to manage sensory sensitivities and improve independence in daily activities.

– Applied Behavior Analysts (ABAs):

ABAs specialize in behavioral interventions. They employ evidence-based techniques to modify behavior, teach new skills, and reduce challenging behaviors in individuals with ASD.

– Special Education Teachers:

Special education teachers design and implement individualized education plans (IEPs) to support the academic, social, and emotional needs of students with ASD. They adapt teaching methods to accommodate diverse learning styles.

– Social Workers and Counselors:

Social workers and counselors offer emotional support and guidance to individuals with ASD and their families. They assist in accessing community resources, coping with stress, and navigating social challenges.

– Rehabilitation Specialists:

Rehabilitation specialists aid in developing life skills, mobility, and independence. They focus on improving functional abilities to foster greater autonomy.

– Behavioral and Developmental Pediatric Teams:

These multidisciplinary teams collaborate to provide comprehensive assessments and interventions. They coordinate care, share insights, and collectively design treatment plans tailored to the individual's needs.

– Care Coordinators and Case Managers:

Care coordinators and case managers facilitate access to services, coordinate care between professionals, and assist families in navigating the complex healthcare system.

Understanding the diverse roles and contributions of these professionals is fundamental in creating a supportive network that addresses the multifaceted needs of individuals with ASD, offering a holistic approach to their care and development.

Assessments and Criteria

The process of diagnosing Autism Spectrum Disorder (ASD) involves comprehensive assessments and specific criteria used by professionals to evaluate and determine if an individual meets the criteria for ASD. Understanding the assessment methods and diagnostic criteria is crucial in recognizing and supporting individuals with ASD.

– Diagnostic Assessments:

Diagnostic assessments involve a multidisciplinary approach where healthcare professionals, including psychologists, pediatricians, and speech-language pathologists, conduct thorough evaluations. These assessments typically encompass observations, interviews, developmental history reviews, and standardized testing to assess social communication, behavior, and developmental milestones.

– DSM-5 Criteria:

The Diagnostic and Statistical Manual of Mental Disorders (DSM-5) is a widely used diagnostic manual that outlines the criteria for diagnosing ASD. It includes two core domains: persistent deficits in social communication and social interaction, and restricted, repetitive patterns of behavior, interests, or activities. These criteria aid professionals in making accurate diagnoses.

– ADOS and ADI-R:

The Autism Diagnostic Observation Schedule (ADOS) and the Autism Diagnostic Interview-Revised (ADI-R) are structured assessments often used in diagnosing ASD. These tools help in observing and evaluating social communication, repetitive behaviors, and social interaction, providing valuable information for diagnosis.

– Developmental and Behavioral Assessments:

Developmental and behavioral assessments focus on evaluating language development, cognitive abilities, adaptive functioning, sensory processing, and motor skills. These assessments assist in understanding an individual's strengths and challenges, aiding in tailored interventions and support strategies.

– Screening Tools:

Screening tools like the M-CHAT (Modified Checklist for Autism in Toddlers) are brief questionnaires designed to identify early signs of ASD in young children. While they do not provide a definitive diagnosis, they flag potential areas that warrant further evaluation.

– Clinical Observation and Parental Reports:

Clinical observation involves assessing behaviors in various settings to understand an individual's social interactions, communication patterns, and repetitive behaviors. Parental reports and input are also crucial, providing valuable insights into a child's behavior and development across different environments.

– Differential Diagnosis:

Differential diagnosis involves distinguishing ASD from other developmental disorders or conditions that might present similar symptoms. It requires a comprehensive evaluation and consideration of medical, neurological, and genetic factors.

Understanding the various assessment methods and diagnostic criteria empowers families, educators, and healthcare professionals to identify ASD early, facilitating timely interventions and appropriate support tailored to the individual's needs.

Chapter 5: Causes and Risk Factors of Autism

This chapter navigates the intricate landscape of Autism Spectrum Disorder's (ASD) origins, focusing on the interplay of genetic, environmental influences, and the pivotal role of neurobiology. Through the lens of scientific exploration, we'll delve into how genetic and environmental elements intertwine to shape ASD. Additionally, we'll unravel the critical role that neurobiology plays in understanding the complexities of autism. From established theories to the latest research advancements, this chapter aims to present a concise overview of the ongoing quest to unravel the factors contributing to ASD, fostering a better comprehension for beginners.

Genetic and Environmental Influences

ASD, a neurodevelopmental condition, emerges from a complex interplay of genetic predispositions and environmental factors. Genetic underpinnings of ASD exhibit a multifaceted landscape, involving a mosaic of genes that, while not individually deterministic, collectively contribute to ASD susceptibility. Researchers have identified multiple genetic variations potentially linked to ASD, revealing the intricate nature of its genetic origins. These variations, often interacting in intricate ways, contribute to the heterogeneity within the ASD spectrum, giving rise to diverse phenotypes and presentations. Concurrently, environmental influences—especially during critical developmental stages—exert notable impact. Prenatal and early childhood environments, encompassing maternal health, prenatal stress, exposure to environmental toxins, and early-life experiences, might shape ASD risk. The intersection of genetic predispositions and environmental influences further complicates the understanding of ASD's etiology. This intricate interaction, where genes and environmental factors converge, remains a focal point of ongoing research endeavors. Unraveling this complex interplay holds promise for better comprehending the nuanced origins of ASD and underpins efforts to formulate personalized interventions and support strategies for individuals along the autism spectrum, aiming for enhanced quality of life and comprehensive care.

The Role of Neurobiology

Understanding Autism Spectrum Disorder (ASD) involves exploring the intricate neurological aspects influencing behavior and development. Neurobiology, the study of the nervous system and its components, contributes significantly to the understanding of ASD. Within the realm of neurobiology, numerous factors are believed to shape the diverse spectrum of characteristics observed in individuals with ASD.

At the core of neurobiological considerations in ASD lies altered brain connectivity and neural pathways. These deviations impact information processing, sensory perception, and social interactions. Evidence suggests that during crucial stages of early brain development, certain neural circuits and synaptic connections may form differently in individuals with ASD. These atypical neural networks can affect how individuals process information, perceive sensory stimuli, and engage in social interactions.

Moreover, researchers have investigated neurotransmitters and their roles in regulating brain function and behavior. Imbalances in neurotransmitters such as serotonin and gamma-aminobutyric acid (GABA) have been associated with challenges in mood regulation, anxiety, and sensory sensitivities often observed in individuals with ASD. This imbalance might contribute to variations in how individuals with ASD experience and respond to their environment.

Advancements in neuroimaging techniques, like functional magnetic resonance imaging (fMRI) and electroencephalography (EEG), have offered glimpses into the neurological underpinnings of ASD. These technologies provide insights into brain activity and connectivity patterns, aiding in understanding how differences in brain structure and function relate to the behavioral manifestations of ASD.

Genetic factors also play a substantial role. While not a singular cause, genetic predispositions contribute to the complex neurological landscape of ASD. Variations in certain genes can influence brain development, synaptic function, and neurotransmitter activity, potentially increasing the likelihood of ASD.

However, despite these insights, unraveling the complete role of neurobiology in ASD remains a complex ongoing endeavor. Understanding the intricate relationships between brain biology, behavior, and environmental factors is crucial in developing tailored interventions and support strategies for individuals on the autism spectrum.

Current Research and Findings

Autism Spectrum Disorder (ASD) is a complex neurodevelopmental condition influenced by a combination of genetic, environmental, and neurological factors. Recent research has been instrumental in elucidating various causes and risk factors associated with ASD.

— **Genetic Research and Hereditary Factors:** Genetic studies have played a significant role in understanding ASD. Research indicates a strong hereditary component, highlighting the influence of genetics in ASD development. Studies have identified numerous genetic variations and mutations, some of which increase the susceptibility to ASD. Recent advancements in genomic sequencing techniques have allowed for the identification of specific genetic markers associated with ASD.

— **Environmental Influences and Epigenetics:** Emerging research suggests that environmental factors during early development might contribute to the risk of ASD. Prenatal and perinatal exposures to factors such as maternal infections, certain medications, toxins, and prenatal stress have been studied for their potential role in ASD onset. Additionally, investigations into epigenetic modifications—changes in gene expression caused by environmental factors—have gained attention as a possible link to ASD.

— **Neurobiological Factors and Brain Development:** Current research focuses on understanding the neurobiological underpinnings of ASD. Studies using advanced neuroimaging techniques have revealed differences in brain structure, connectivity, and function in individuals with ASD. These findings indicate altered brain development and connectivity patterns, suggesting a neurological basis for certain ASD characteristics.

– **Immune System and Inflammation:** Research exploring the relationship between immune system dysregulation and ASD has gained momentum. Studies have shown associations between immune dysfunction, inflammatory responses, and ASD. Investigations into maternal immune activation and its impact on fetal development, as well as abnormalities in immune markers in individuals with ASD, have contributed to understanding the immune-inflammatory component of ASD.

– **Gut Microbiota and Metabolic Factors:** Recent studies have investigated the gut-brain connection and its potential influence on ASD. Alterations in gut microbiota composition, gastrointestinal symptoms, and metabolic differences have been observed in individuals with ASD. Research suggests a possible link between gut health, metabolic imbalances, and ASD symptoms, although the precise mechanisms require further exploration.

– **Risk Factors and Early Indicators:** Ongoing research focuses on identifying early indicators and risk factors for ASD. Studies aim to identify predictive markers, such as early behavioral signs or biological markers, that could aid in early detection and intervention. Understanding these risk factors could potentially lead to earlier interventions and improved outcomes for individuals with ASD.

As research in the field of ASD continues to evolve, these ongoing investigations and findings provide crucial insights into the multifaceted nature of the causes and risk factors associated with Autism Spectrum Disorder.

Chapter 6: Approaches to Support and Therapy

Chapter 6, "Approaches to Support and Therapy," delves into various strategies essential for supporting individuals with Autism Spectrum Disorder (ASD). This chapter is divided into three key sections: Therapeutic Interventions and Treatments, which explore evidence-based therapies targeting specific ASD challenges; Behavioral and Communication Strategies, focusing on practical approaches to managing behaviors and enhancing communication skills; and Alternative and Complementary Therapies, discussing non-conventional methods that complement traditional interventions, providing a broader spectrum of support options. Each section aims to empower readers by offering a diverse toolkit of strategies to enhance the lives of individuals with ASD, catering to their unique needs and fostering a better understanding of effective support methods.

Therapeutic Interventions and Treatments

Therapeutic interventions and treatments for Autism Spectrum Disorder (ASD) encompass a range of evidence-based approaches tailored to address various challenges and improve the quality of life for individuals on the spectrum. Understanding and utilizing these interventions play a crucial role in supporting individuals with ASD.

– Applied Behavior Analysis (ABA)

Applied Behavior Analysis (ABA) is a widely recognized and extensively researched intervention for individuals with ASD. It focuses on understanding behavior and employs techniques to encourage positive behaviors and discourage negative ones. ABA involves breaking down complex skills into smaller, manageable steps, utilizing reinforcement strategies to facilitate learning. This structured approach helps individuals develop communication, social, and daily living skills.

– Speech and Language Therapy

Speech and language therapy aims to enhance communication abilities in individuals with ASD. Therapists use various techniques to improve speech clarity, language comprehension, and social communication skills. These therapies may include augmentative and alternative communication (AAC) strategies, sign language, picture exchange systems, and other assistive technologies to support communication development.

– Occupational Therapy (OT)

Occupational therapy focuses on improving an individual's ability to participate in daily activities and enhances skills related to sensory processing, motor coordination, self-care, and adaptive behaviors. Occupational therapists develop personalized interventions to address sensory sensitivities, motor skills deficits, and difficulties with daily routines, aiming to improve independence and functional abilities.

– Social Skills Training

Social skills training programs help individuals with ASD develop and refine social interaction abilities. These programs employ structured sessions to teach social cues, conversation skills, perspective-taking, and appropriate social behaviors in various settings. Role-playing exercises and group activities facilitate the practice of these skills in real-life situations.

– Cognitive Behavioral Therapy (CBT)

Cognitive Behavioral Therapy (CBT) assists individuals in managing emotions, reducing anxiety, and addressing behavioral challenges associated with ASD. This therapy helps identify and modify negative thought patterns and behaviors by teaching coping strategies, problem-solving techniques, and emotion regulation skills.

– Sensory Integration Therapy

For individuals with sensory sensitivities or difficulties processing sensory information, sensory integration therapy provides techniques to manage sensory overload or under-responsiveness. Occupational therapists employ sensory-rich activities to help individuals regulate sensory input, improving tolerance to different sensations and environments.

– Developmental and Relationship-Based Therapies

Developmental and relationship-based therapies emphasize fostering meaningful connections and relationships. Therapists focus on building emotional connections, promoting joint attention, and enhancing reciprocal communication between individuals with ASD and their caregivers or peers.

– Pharmacological Interventions

In some cases, healthcare professionals may prescribe medications to manage specific symptoms associated with ASD, such as anxiety, attention deficits, or aggression. However, medication interventions are typically tailored to address individual needs and are carefully monitored by healthcare providers.

Therapeutic interventions and treatments for ASD offer a spectrum of approaches aimed at addressing diverse challenges individuals with autism face. These interventions, often used in combination, provide comprehensive support to enhance communication, social skills, behavior management, and overall quality of life for individuals on the autism spectrum. The effectiveness of each intervention may vary for each individual, highlighting the importance of personalized and multidisciplinary approaches in supporting those with ASD.

Behavioral and Communication Strategies

Autism Spectrum Disorder (ASD) often presents with diverse behavioral patterns. It's crucial to recognize these behaviors, which might include repetitive actions, difficulty in social interactions, and sensory sensitivities. Understanding these patterns allows for tailored strategies to support individuals with ASD effectively.

– Applied Behavior Analysis (ABA) Explained

Applied Behavior Analysis (ABA) is a structured approach widely used for individuals with ASD. It involves breaking down tasks into smaller components, using positive reinforcement to encourage desired behaviors, and addressing challenging behaviors through systematic plans. ABA aims to teach new skills and modify behaviors effectively.

– Picture Exchange Communication System (PECS) for Communication

The Picture Exchange Communication System (PECS) is a visual communication tool beneficial for non-verbal or minimally verbal individuals. PECS utilizes images or symbols exchanged to express needs or desires, facilitating communication development and enhancing social interactions.

– Social Stories and Visual Supports

Social Stories and Visual Supports play a pivotal role in aiding individuals with ASD to understand social cues, routines, and appropriate behaviors. Social Stories use simple narratives with visuals to explain social situations, while Visual Supports include visual aids like schedules or charts to structure tasks and routines effectively.

Augmentative and Alternative Communication (AAC) Methods

Augmentative and Alternative Communication (AAC) methods offer alternative ways to communicate beyond speech. AAC tools include communication boards, sign language, or devices that generate speech. Implementing the appropriate AAC method depends on an individual's communication needs and abilities.

– Strategies for Managing Sensory Sensitivities

Sensory sensitivities are common in ASD. Strategies to manage these sensitivities include creating sensory-friendly environments, providing sensory-focused activities, utilizing tools like headphones or fidget toys, and introducing sensory breaks when needed.

– Behavioral Modification Techniques

Behavioral modification techniques, such as using rewards, setting up structured routines, and implementing clear and consistent rules, help shape positive behaviors and reduce challenging ones. Positive reinforcement plays a key role in encouraging desired behaviors.

– Developing Social Skills through Structured Activities

To foster social skills, structured activities like role-playing scenarios, peer-based interactions, and social skills training programs are beneficial. These activities aim to improve social understanding, perspective-taking, and building meaningful relationships.

Alternative and Complementary Therapies

Alternative and complementary therapies encompass a wide array of non-traditional interventions designed to complement conventional treatments for individuals with Autism Spectrum Disorder (ASD). While these therapies vary in their approaches, they often aim to address specific symptoms, enhance well-being, and offer additional support for individuals with ASD.

Types of Alternative and Complementary Therapies

- **Music Therapy**

Music therapy involves the use of music to address emotional, social, and communication difficulties commonly observed in individuals with ASD. It utilizes structured musical activities to promote relaxation, improve social interaction, and foster emotional expression.

- **Art Therapy**

Art therapy focuses on using artistic activities as a means of expression and communication for individuals with ASD. Through various art forms, such as painting, drawing, or sculpting, it allows individuals to convey their emotions and thoughts, aiding in emotional regulation and social connection.

- **Animal-Assisted Therapy (AAT)**

AAT involves interactions between individuals with ASD and trained animals, such as dogs or horses. These interactions aim to improve social skills, reduce anxiety, and enhance emotional well-being through the therapeutic bond formed with animals.

- **Sensory Integration Therapy**

Sensory integration therapy targets sensory processing difficulties commonly associated with ASD. It involves structured activities that aim to regulate sensory responses, improve tolerance to sensory stimuli, and enhance overall sensory processing.

- **Yoga and Mindfulness**

Practices like yoga and mindfulness techniques have shown promise in supporting individuals with ASD. These practices focus on relaxation, breathing exercises, and mindfulness, aiming to reduce anxiety, improve attention, and promote self-regulation.

Evidence and Considerations

While some alternative and complementary therapies have gained popularity, their effectiveness varies, and evidence supporting their use for individuals with ASD can be limited or mixed. It's crucial for caregivers and individuals to consider the following:

- Scientific Evidence: Review existing research and consult healthcare professionals to understand the potential benefits and limitations of each therapy.
- Individualized Approach: Recognize that each individual with ASD is unique; what works for one person may not work for another. Tailor therapies to suit individual needs and preferences.
- Integration with Conventional Treatments: These therapies should complement, not replace, evidence-based interventions. Integrating them into a comprehensive treatment plan under professional guidance

can offer holistic support.

Alternative and complementary therapies present a diverse range of options to support individuals with ASD. While some may offer benefits in specific areas, it's essential to approach these therapies critically, considering individual needs and scientific evidence, and integrating them into a broader, evidence-based treatment framework.

Chapter 7: Nurturing Communication and Social Skills

This chapter delves into pivotal aspects of fostering communication and social skills in individuals with Autism Spectrum Disorder (ASD). It aims to address various challenges faced in communication, offer strategies for enhancement, explore the nuances of social interaction, emphasize the importance of building relationships, and highlight methods for supporting emotional regulation. Subsequent sections will delve into Communication Challenges and Enhancements, Social Interaction and Building Relationships, and Supporting Emotional Regulation to provide a comprehensive understanding and actionable insights in aiding individuals with ASD in these vital areas of development.

Communication Challenges and Enhancements

Communication plays a pivotal role in our daily lives, serving as a means to express thoughts, emotions, and needs. For individuals on the Autism Spectrum, communication can present various challenges due to differences in processing, social interaction, and sensory integration. Understanding these challenges and exploring enhancement strategies is crucial in facilitating effective communication.

> Communication Challenges :

- Verbal Communication Difficulties

Many individuals with Autism may experience challenges in verbal communication, such as delayed language development, limited vocabulary, or echolalia (repeating words or phrases).

- Non-Verbal Communication Differences

Non-verbal communication, including body language, facial expressions, and gestures, might be challenging for some individuals with Autism, leading to difficulties in understanding or expressing non-verbal cues.

- Social Communication Deficits

Difficulties in understanding social nuances, initiating or maintaining conversations, and comprehending abstract or figurative language are common challenges faced in social communication by individuals on the Autism Spectrum.

- Sensory Sensitivities Impacting Communication

Sensory sensitivities can significantly affect communication. Over or under-sensitivity to sensory stimuli (like sound, touch, or light) might cause distress and interfere with communication attempts.

> Enhancement Strategies :

- Visual Supports and Augmentative Communication

Visual supports, such as picture communication systems, visual schedules, or PECS (Picture Exchange Communication System), can assist in enhancing communication by providing visual cues and aids.

- Social Skills Training

Targeted social skills training programs can help individuals with Autism to understand social cues, improve conversation initiation, turn-taking, and comprehension of social expectations.

- Use of Assistive Technology

Technology-based aids, like speech-generating devices, tablets with communication apps, or text-to-speech software, can aid in communication, especially for non-verbal individuals or those with limited speech.

- Applied Behavioral Analysis (ABA)

ABA techniques, including discrete trial teaching, pivotal response training, and behavior modification, are employed to enhance communication skills by reinforcing desired behaviors.

- Sensory Integration Techniques

Implementing sensory integration therapies and techniques can address sensory sensitivities, minimizing their impact on communication abilities.

Recognizing the communication challenges faced by individuals on the Autism Spectrum is crucial for implementing effective strategies and interventions to enhance communication skills. Through the application of various approaches tailored to individual needs, it's possible to support and improve communication for individuals with Autism, fostering their interaction and connection with the world around them.

Social Interaction and Building Relationships

Social interaction and establishing meaningful relationships are fundamental aspects of human life. Individuals on the Autism Spectrum often encounter distinctive challenges in navigating social situations and forming connections. Understanding these challenges and exploring strategies to foster social interaction and relationship-building is crucial for their holistic development.

> **Unique Challenges in Social Interaction**

- Navigating Social Norms and Context

Understanding unwritten social rules, interpreting nuanced social cues, and comprehending the context of different social settings can be challenging for individuals on the Autism Spectrum.

- Difficulty in Forming Reciprocal Relationships

Building and maintaining reciprocal relationships can be challenging due to difficulties in understanding the give-and-take nature of social interactions, leading to potential social isolation.

- Struggling with Social Flexibility

Rigidity in thought patterns or adherence to routine can hinder adaptability in social situations, making it challenging to adjust behaviors or responses according to social demands.

- Managing Anxiety in Social Scenarios

Anxiety stemming from unfamiliar or overwhelming social situations can significantly impact an individual's ability to engage comfortably and participate in social interactions.

> **Strategies for Enhancing Social Skills**

- Social Skill Development Programs

Targeted programs focusing on social skills development, including understanding emotions, perspective-taking, and practicing social scenarios, can aid in navigating various social settings effectively.

- Utilizing Visual Supports and Social Scripts

Employing visual aids, social scripts, or role-playing activities can assist in explaining social expectations, steps for social interactions, or handling specific social situations.

- Encouraging Peer Involvement and Socialization

Encouraging interactions with neurotypical peers through structured activities or peer-mediated interventions can provide opportunities for practicing social skills in natural social settings.

- Structured Social Groups and Shared Activities

Engaging in structured group activities aligned with their interests can provide a conducive environment for individuals with autism to interact, share experiences, and develop social connections.

- Emphasizing Shared Interests and Hobbies

Encouraging and facilitating involvement in hobbies and interests can serve as a platform for initiating and nurturing social connections with like-minded individuals.

> **Building Meaningful Relationships**

- Teaching Empathy and Understanding Emotions

Fostering empathy, understanding others' perspectives, and recognizing emotions can contribute to the development of meaningful and reciprocal relationships.

- Enhancing Communication Strategies

Emphasizing clear communication strategies, such as expressing needs, emotions, and boundaries effectively, is vital for building and sustaining healthy relationships.

- Promoting Independence and Self-Advocacy

Encouraging self-advocacy, independence, and decision-making skills empowers individuals with autism to navigate social interactions confidently.

Navigating social interactions and establishing relationships poses significant challenges for individuals on the Autism Spectrum. Implementing tailored strategies, focusing on social skill development, and fostering meaningful connections within diverse social contexts are crucial in facilitating their social growth and improving their quality of life.

Supporting Emotional Regulation

Emotional regulation is the ability to understand, manage, and express emotions effectively. Individuals on the Autism Spectrum may encounter unique challenges in regulating their emotions due to sensory sensitivities, difficulty understanding emotions, and navigating social interactions. This chapter explores strategies tailored specifically to support emotional regulation for individuals with autism.

> **Unique Challenges in Emotional Regulation**

- Sensory Sensitivities and Emotional Responses

Sensory sensitivities prevalent in autism can trigger intense emotional reactions, causing emotional dysregulation in response to overwhelming sensory input.

- Difficulty Identifying and Expressing Emotions

Some individuals with autism experience challenges in accurately recognizing and articulating their emotions, hindering their ability to regulate them effectively.

- Anxiety from Changes and Uncertainty

Situational changes or unpredictability can induce anxiety and emotional distress for individuals with autism, impacting their emotional regulation.

- Social Interaction and Emotional Regulation

Misinterpretation of social cues or difficulties in social interactions can lead to emotional stress and challenges in regulating emotions appropriately.

> **Tailored Strategies for Support**

- Sensory Regulation Techniques

Implementing sensory-friendly environments, offering sensory tools, and incorporating regular sensory breaks aids in managing emotions triggered by sensory sensitivities.

- Visual Supports for Emotions

Utilizing visual aids, like emotion charts or emotion cards, assists individuals in identifying and expressing their feelings, facilitating emotional regulation.

- Mindfulness and Relaxation Practices

Teaching mindfulness exercises, deep breathing techniques, or guided relaxation helps manage emotional responses and promotes self-regulation.

- Structured Routines and Predictability

Maintaining consistent routines and schedules provides a sense of security, reducing emotional distress caused by unexpected changes.

- Individualized Coping Strategies

Encouraging the development of personalized coping mechanisms empowers individuals to manage emotional challenges effectively.

> **Empowering Self-Advocacy and Support Systems**

- Self-Advocacy Skills Development

Supporting individuals to express their emotions and advocate for their needs enhances their emotional well-being and self-regulation.

- Building Positive Support Networks

Fostering supportive relationships and social connections creates a safe space for emotional expression and seeking help when needed.

Emotional regulation is pivotal for overall well-being, particularly for individuals on the Autism Spectrum. By implementing tailored strategies that address sensory sensitivities, emotional recognition, and coping mechanisms, vital support can be provided to enhance emotional regulation skills and promote emotional well-being.

Chapter 8: Education and Learning Strategies

This chapter delves into the critical realm of education and learning strategies tailored for individuals within the Autism Spectrum. It examines fundamental aspects such as educational rights, Individualized Education Plans (IEPs), classroom accommodations, and post-school options for transitioning to adulthood. Subsections will focus on outlining the rights of individuals in educational settings, accommodations needed within the classroom environment, and the various options available as individuals transition into adult life post-schooling.

Educational Rights and Individualized Education Plans (IEPs)

Education is a fundamental right for every individual, and for children with autism, accessing quality education tailored to their unique needs is imperative for their development. Understanding the educational rights and the formulation of Individualized Education Plans (IEPs) ensures that these individuals receive appropriate support and resources within the educational system.

- **Understanding Educational Rights:**

The journey toward advocating for the educational needs of individuals with autism begins with understanding their rights. In many countries, there are specific laws and regulations, such as the Individuals with Disabilities Education Act (IDEA) in the United States, that safeguard the rights of children with disabilities, including autism, to receive a free and appropriate public education (FAPE). These laws ensure access to specialized services, accommodations, and resources necessary for effective learning. Knowing these rights empowers parents, caregivers, educators, and advocates in advocating for the best possible educational experience for children on the autism spectrum.

- **The Role of Individualized Education Plans (IEPs):**

At the heart of supporting children with autism in the educational setting lies the creation and implementation of Individualized Education Plans (IEPs). An IEP is a personalized blueprint designed to address the specific strengths and challenges of each child. It is developed collaboratively by a team that includes parents, educators, specialists, and sometimes the student, ensuring that it reflects the individual needs, goals, and objectives of the child.

- **Components of an IEP:**

An IEP is a comprehensive document that outlines various elements crucial for the child's educational journey. It includes the child's present levels of academic achievement and functional performance, specific and measurable annual goals, the services and accommodations the child will receive, related services (such as speech therapy or occupational therapy), and a plan for how progress will be measured and reported to parents.

- **Implementing and Monitoring the IEP:**

Once the IEP is established, its successful implementation becomes paramount. Educators and support staff play a vital role in executing the plan within the classroom environment. Ongoing monitoring and periodic reviews are crucial to track the child's progress and make necessary adjustments to the IEP to ensure it remains effective and aligned with the child's evolving needs.

- **Collaboration and Advocacy:**

Collaboration between parents, educators, specialists, and the student is key throughout the IEP process. Encouraging open communication and teamwork fosters a supportive environment that enables the child to thrive academically and socially. Additionally, advocating for the child's needs within the educational system ensures that the IEP remains a dynamic tool aimed at optimizing the child's educational experience.

Understanding educational rights and the development and implementation of Individualized Education Plans (IEPs) are pivotal in ensuring that children with autism receive the necessary support and resources to achieve their full potential within the educational landscape.

Classroom Accommodations and Modifications

Students with autism often benefit from specific accommodations and modifications in the classroom environment to facilitate their learning experiences. Understanding and implementing these adjustments can significantly enhance their educational journey.

- **Understanding Classroom Accommodations and Modifications:**

Understanding Classroom Accommodations and Modifications encompasses a multifaceted approach tailored to meet the diverse and specific needs of students with autism within the educational setting. It involves a comprehensive evaluation of individual strengths, challenges, and learning styles, necessitating collaboration among educators, parents, specialists, and the student. These adaptations span various domains, including sensory considerations to create a comfortable learning environment, implementation of visual aids and schedules to enhance comprehension and structure, incorporation of flexible teaching methods to accommodate diverse learning styles, and establishment of consistent routines for predictability. Additionally, adjustments such as alternative seating arrangements, quiet spaces, and tools for sensory regulation contribute to an inclusive atmosphere. This process requires a keen understanding of each student's unique profile, fostering an inclusive educational environment that supports academic achievement, social interaction, and overall well-being for students with autism.

- **Creating an Inclusive Environment:**

Creating an inclusive environment within educational settings for students with autism involves fostering an atmosphere that not only accepts but celebrates diversity. It necessitates an active commitment to understanding, respecting, and valuing individual differences. This begins with promoting awareness and empathy among peers, educators, and staff members, cultivating an environment where every student feels welcomed, respected, and supported. Strategies encompass encouraging positive peer interactions, fostering a culture of acceptance through education and discussions about neurodiversity, promoting teamwork and collaboration among students, and implementing anti-bullying policies that emphasize kindness and empathy. Furthermore, it involves physical and sensory adjustments, including flexible seating arrangements, quiet areas for relaxation or sensory regulation, and ensuring adequate lighting and minimal distractions. Educators and school leadership play a pivotal role by providing ongoing training to staff, promoting a mindset of inclusivity, and advocating for inclusive practices throughout the institution. Creating an inclusive environment isn't a singular action but an ongoing commitment that requires dedication, understanding, and a collective effort to create a supportive and nurturing space where all students, including those with autism, can thrive socially, emotionally, and academically.

- **Adapting Teaching Strategies:**

Adapting teaching strategies for students with autism is a multifaceted process aimed at catering to diverse learning styles and individual needs within the classroom. This involves a flexible and personalized approach that acknowledges the unique strengths, challenges, and sensory preferences of each student. Educators employ a variety of methods such as visual supports, structured routines, multisensory learning activities, and differentiated instruction to accommodate different learning preferences. Visual aids, including visual schedules, charts, and diagrams, help in providing clarity and structure, while structured routines contribute to predictability and reduce anxiety. Furthermore, incorporating hands-on activities, interactive lessons, and incorporating technology into the curriculum enhance engagement and facilitate comprehension. Flexibility in teaching methods allows educators to adapt lessons based on individual responses, providing additional support or accommodations as needed. Ultimately, by embracing varied teaching strategies, educators create an inclusive environment that fosters academic growth and supports the diverse needs of students with autism.

- **Environmental Modifications:**

Physical adjustments in the classroom environment can significantly impact students with autism. Exploring environmental modifications includes creating sensory-friendly spaces, minimizing sensory distractions, providing sensory tools (like fidget toys or noise-canceling headphones), offering flexible seating arrangements, and utilizing calming areas for students who may need a break.

- **Supporting Social and Emotional Learning:**

Social and emotional skills are vital for students with autism. Strategies to support social interaction, communication, and emotional regulation within the classroom encompass social skills training, peer mentoring programs, emotional regulation techniques, and promoting understanding of emotions through social stories or role-playing scenarios.

- **Individualized Support Plans:**

Adapting teaching strategies to fit individualized support plans is crucial for helping students with autism in their learning journey. These personalized plans, like Individualized Education Plans (IEPs) or Behavior Intervention Plans (BIPs), are created together with teachers, parents, specialists, and the student. They're like personalized roadmaps designed to help students reach their specific goals in school. Teachers use these plans to bring special teaching methods, behavioral tips, and necessary changes to the classroom. They're like a guide that helps teachers support students better, track their progress, and make sure they're doing well in their studies and in how they feel at school. By using these plans, teachers can create a welcoming and supportive learning space that helps students with autism learn and grow at their own pace.

- **Collaboration and Professional Development:**

Collaboration among educators and ongoing professional development are super important for helping students with autism. It's like teamwork where teachers, specialists, and other school staff work together, sharing ideas and strategies to support these students better. When everyone works as a team, it helps in understanding more about autism and the best ways to help students learn. Also, teachers keep learning new things through professional development—like special training or workshops—that teach them more about autism and how to use different teaching methods. This learning helps teachers discover new ways to create a classroom where all students, including those with autism, feel welcome and supported. Through teamwork and continued learning, teachers become better at providing the right kind of help and creating a great school environment for everyone to learn together.

Implementing effective classroom accommodations and modifications is a collaborative effort that involves understanding individual needs, implementing targeted strategies, and creating an inclusive learning environment where all students, including those with autism, can thrive academically and socially.

Transitioning to Adulthood: Post-School Options

Transitioning from school to adulthood can be both exciting and challenging for individuals with autism. This crucial phase involves navigating various options and support systems to ensure a smooth transition towards independent living, employment, further education, and community integration.

- **Understanding the Transition Process:**

The transition from school to adulthood is a significant milestone requiring careful planning and preparation. This phase typically begins around the age of 14-16, focusing on identifying the individual's strengths, preferences, interests, and goals. It involves collaborating with educators, families, specialists, and community resources to develop a comprehensive transition plan.

- **Exploring Post-School Options:**

– Employment Opportunities: Exploring employment options is crucial. This includes vocational training, job coaching, supported employment programs, internships, and job placements aimed at matching skills and interests to suitable career paths.

– Continuing Education: Some individuals may opt for further education after high school. Colleges and vocational training institutes often offer programs tailored to accommodate diverse learning styles, providing academic and life skills support.

– Independent Living Support: Transitioning to independent living involves learning life skills such as managing finances, transportation, cooking, and accessing community resources. Supportive housing programs or transitional living arrangements can assist individuals in this transition.

– Community Engagement and Social Inclusion: Engaging in community activities, clubs, and social groups fosters social connections and helps individuals develop friendships and supportive networks beyond school.

- **Support Systems and Resources:**

Navigating post-school options involves accessing various support systems:

– Transition Coordinators: These professionals help develop transition plans, link families to resources, and guide individuals through the transition process.

– Vocational Rehabilitation Services: These services offer career counseling, job training, and placement assistance for individuals with disabilities, supporting their entry into the workforce.

– Community Organizations and Agencies: Non-profit organizations, disability advocacy groups, and government agencies often provide resources, support, and information regarding housing, employment, healthcare, and legal rights.

- **Legal and Financial Planning:**

Understanding legal and financial matters is essential. This includes exploring guardianship, estate planning, public benefits, and financial support programs available for individuals with disabilities to ensure their long-term well-being and security.

- **Empowerment and Self-Advocacy:**

Empowering individuals with autism involves fostering self-advocacy skills. Encouraging them to voice their preferences, make informed decisions, and participate actively in planning their future enhances their autonomy and confidence.

Transitioning to adulthood and exploring post-school options for individuals with autism requires a comprehensive approach involving collaboration, planning, and access to diverse resources. By facilitating a seamless transition and empowering individuals with the necessary skills and support, we can assist them in achieving greater independence, meaningful employment, and a fulfilling life in their communities.

Chapter 9: Supporting Individuals with Autism

Chapter 9 delves into the vital support systems essential for individuals with autism. Divided into three key sections, this chapter explores the significant roles played by Family and Community Support (Subchapter A), Advocacy and Empowerment (Subchapter B), and Creating Inclusive Environments (Subchapter C). It outlines the importance of familial and community backing, the advocacy efforts crucial for raising awareness and promoting rights, and the creation of inclusive settings vital for the overall well-being and success of individuals with autism.

Family and Community Support

Support from family and the community plays a crucial role in the holistic development and well-being of individuals with autism. This section focuses on understanding the pivotal role of familial and communal support systems in nurturing and empowering individuals on the autism spectrum.

- **The Power of Family Support:**

Family support serves as the cornerstone in the life of someone with autism. It encompasses emotional support, guidance, and advocacy. Families play a critical role in providing a nurturing environment, understanding individual needs, and fostering a sense of belonging and acceptance. They often seek information, connect with support groups, and actively participate in educational and therapeutic interventions for their loved ones.

- **Community Involvement and Support Networks:**

Communities can significantly impact the lives of individuals with autism. Collaborating with community organizations, support groups, and local services is vital. These connections foster social interactions, access to resources, and a sense of inclusion. Community support networks offer valuable resources such as respite care, specialized programs, and social activities that aid in the overall development and social integration of individuals with autism.

- **Educating and Raising Awareness:**

Educating the community about autism is crucial in creating an inclusive environment. Awareness initiatives, workshops, and campaigns help dispel myths, reduce stigma, and promote understanding. This knowledge empowers communities to create welcoming spaces and support individuals with autism effectively.

- **Addressing Challenges and Celebrating Achievements:**

Families and communities navigate challenges together, addressing issues related to accessibility, inclusion, and advocating for equal opportunities. Celebrating milestones and achievements, no matter how small, contributes to building confidence and fostering a sense of accomplishment among individuals with autism.

- **Collaboration and Empowerment:**

Collaboration between families, community organizations, educational institutions, and policymakers is essential. Empowering families with access to resources, advocating for inclusive policies, and fostering a supportive environment ensures a holistic support system that nurtures the potential of individuals with autism.

In conclusion, family and community support are fundamental pillars in the lives of individuals with autism. They form an integral part of a supportive network that fosters understanding, acceptance, and opportunities for growth, ultimately enabling individuals on the autism spectrum to lead fulfilling lives within their communities.

Advocacy and Empowerment

Advocacy and empowerment are essential pillars in the lives of individuals with autism, ensuring their rights, inclusion, and opportunities for a fulfilling life.

- **Understanding Advocacy:**

Advocacy involves speaking up, promoting, and protecting the rights and needs of individuals with autism. It encompasses various forms, including self-advocacy, where individuals express their own needs and preferences, and external advocacy, where supporters and organizations speak on behalf of those unable to advocate for themselves. Advocacy initiatives aim to raise awareness, influence policies, and create inclusive environments.

- **Empowerment through Education and Awareness:**

Empowerment of individuals with autism begins with education and awareness. It involves equipping them with knowledge about their rights, abilities, and available resources. Educational programs, workshops, and resources focused on autism awareness help empower individuals by providing them with the tools to self-advocate, make informed decisions, and navigate various aspects of life independently.

- **Supporting Self-Advocacy:**

Encouraging self-advocacy is crucial in empowering individuals with autism. It involves fostering their ability to express their needs, preferences, and concerns confidently. Developing communication skills, self-awareness, and self-determination enhances their capability to effectively communicate and assert their rights in various settings.

- **Promoting Inclusivity and Equal Opportunities:**

Advocacy efforts aim to create inclusive environments and advocate for equal opportunities in education, employment, healthcare, and societal participation. This includes pushing for reasonable accommodations, accessibility, anti-discrimination policies, nend fostering a culture of acceptance and understanding.

- **Collaboration and Community Engagement:**

Effective advocacy often involves collaboration with community organizations, policymakers, educators, and healthcare providers. Building partnerships and engaging with stakeholders enable the development and implementation of policies and practices that promote the rights and well-being of individuals with autism.

- **Celebrating Progress and Continuing Efforts:**

Acknowledging achievements in advocacy efforts is crucial. Recognizing successful initiatives, legislative changes, and increased awareness serves as motivation to continue advocating for the rights and empowerment of individuals with autism.

Advocacy and empowerment are integral in ensuring the rights, inclusion, and well-being of individuals with autism. By amplifying their voices, fostering self-advocacy, and creating inclusive environments, we can empower individuals across the autism spectrum to lead fulfilling lives and contribute meaningfully to society.

Creating Inclusive Environments

Creating environments that are truly inclusive for individuals with autism involves a multifaceted approach that addresses various facets to ensure acceptance, accessibility, and support

- **Foundations of Inclusivity:**

Inclusivity begins with an understanding and acceptance of neurodiversity. It involves valuing and respecting individual differences, ensuring that every person, regardless of their abilities or challenges, feels welcome and appreciated. It encompasses recognizing and celebrating the unique strengths and perspectives that each person brings to the community.

- **Designing Physical Spaces for Accessibility:**

Physical spaces are crucial in creating an inclusive environment. Design considerations go beyond mere aesthetics to prioritize accessibility and sensory considerations. Incorporating elements such as sensory-friendly lighting, quiet zones, comfortable seating, and adaptable spaces caters to diverse sensory needs and promotes a sense of safety and ease.

- **Facilitating Social Integration:**

Promoting social interaction and integration is key to inclusivity. Organizing activities that encourage peer-to-peer engagement, group projects, or social clubs can provide opportunities for individuals with autism to interact, build relationships, and feel integrated into the community.

- **Communication and Expression Support:**

Effective communication is fundamental in inclusive environments. Providing various communication aids like visual schedules, picture-based communication systems, and assistive technologies aids individuals with autism in expressing themselves and understanding others effectively.

- **Sensory Accommodations and Supports:**

Inclusive spaces acknowledge and accommodate sensory differences. Implementing measures like noise reduction strategies, access to sensory tools, and allowing breaks in overwhelming situations supports individuals in managing sensory challenges, fostering a more comfortable environment.

- **Professional Training and Education:**

Educating and training professionals, caregivers, and support staff in autism awareness and best practices is vital. This training equips them with the tools to understand diverse needs and implement strategies that cater to the individual requirements of those with autism.

- **Community Engagement and Partnerships:**

Collaborating with the broader community is crucial for creating a truly inclusive environment. Engaging local businesses, community groups, and service providers fosters a supportive network that extends beyond specific educational or care settings.

- **Celebrating Diversity and Achievements:**

Inclusive environments celebrate diversity and individual accomplishments. Recognizing and acknowledging achievements, milestones, and unique talents of individuals with autism contributes to a culture of acceptance and appreciation.

Crafting inclusive environments for individuals with autism requires a holistic and tailored approach that encompasses physical, social, sensory, and educational aspects. By embracing diversity, understanding unique needs, and providing necessary support, these environments facilitate growth, learning, and a sense of belonging for everyone.

Chapter 10: Thriving on the Spectrum: Celebrating Strengths

This chapter is a celebration of the unique strengths and talents found within the autism spectrum. It explores how embracing neurodiversity fosters an appreciation for the diverse abilities of individuals on the spectrum. Through stories of success and role models, it highlights the remarkable accomplishments and contributions made by individuals with autism.

Unique Abilities and Talents

Welcome to the extraordinary world of unique abilities and talents found in individuals on the autism spectrum. Let's embark on a journey to discover the remarkable skills that make each person on the spectrum truly exceptional.

- **Extraordinary Talents:**

Individuals on the autism spectrum possess incredible talents and abilities that set them apart. Some have exceptional memory skills, allowing them to remember vast amounts of information or recall intricate details. Others showcase remarkable creativity through their artistic talents, painting vivid pictures or playing beautiful music.

- **Specialized Interests:**

Many individuals with autism develop intense interests in particular topics. They might become experts in fields like astronomy, trains, or computers, diving deep into these subjects and gathering extensive knowledge. These interests often transform into extraordinary skills or hobbies.

- **Remarkable Attention to Detail:**

People on the autism spectrum often pay close attention to details that others might overlook. This attention to detail can be incredibly helpful in various activities, such as finding mistakes in complex puzzles or observing intricate patterns in nature.

Unique Thinking Patterns:

Some individuals with autism think differently, allowing them to see connections or patterns that others might miss. This kind of thinking can lead to innovative problem-solving approaches and creative solutions in various situations.

- **Encouraging and Supporting Talents:**

Recognizing and supporting these amazing abilities is crucial. Providing opportunities for individuals to develop and use their unique talents not only helps them grow but also enables others to appreciate and learn from their exceptional skills.

- **Celebrating Diversity:**

We celebrate these unique abilities! Embracing and encouraging these talents fosters an inclusive environment where everyone's differences are valued and respected. By recognizing and appreciating diverse talents, we create a society that embraces uniqueness and diversity.

The exceptional abilities and talents exhibited by individuals on the autism spectrum are a source of inspiration and uniqueness. Embracing and nurturing these talents enriches the lives of individuals and contributes to a more understanding and inclusive society.

Embracing Neurodiversity

Neurodiversity is the recognition that each individual's brain functions uniquely. It celebrates the diversity of human minds, acknowledging that differences in cognition are natural and valuable aspects of the human experience.

- **Understanding Neurodiversity:**

Neurodiversity encompasses a spectrum of cognitive differences, including conditions such as autism, ADHD, dyslexia, and more. It emphasizes that these differences are not merely deficits but offer distinct strengths and perspectives.

- **Appreciating Cognitive Differences:**

Embracing neurodiversity involves appreciating the multitude of cognitive perspectives present in our society. Individuals with neurodiverse traits may possess heightened creativity, exceptional attention to detail, remarkable problem-solving abilities, or deep passion for specific subjects.

- **Challenging Prejudice and Stigma:**

By promoting neurodiversity, we challenge societal stigmas and misconceptions. It aims to break down stereotypes that view neurodivergent traits solely as shortcomings, fostering a more inclusive and accepting environment.

- **Supporting Inclusion and Acceptance:**

Creating inclusive spaces involves understanding and accommodating diverse cognitive needs. It's about providing reasonable accommodations and support, ensuring equal opportunities for all individuals to contribute and thrive.

- **Education and Awareness:**

Raising awareness about neurodiversity fosters understanding, empathy, and acceptance. Educating society about the strengths and challenges of neurodiverse individuals is key to creating a more empathetic and supportive community.

- **Valuing Diversity of Thought:**

Embracing neurodiversity encourages us to value diverse ways of thinking, problem-solving, and learning. It underscores the importance of creating environments that embrace different cognitive styles, allowing each person to flourish.

In essence, embracing neurodiversity is about recognizing and celebrating the unique cognitive strengths and differences within humanity. It involves fostering inclusive environments, advocating for acceptance, and appreciating the multitude of ways individuals perceive and interact with the world.

Success Stories and Role Models

Within the vast spectrum of human diversity lies a tapestry of remarkable individuals whose stories illuminate resilience, tenacity, and unparalleled talent. This section is a celebration of these shining stars within the autism community, individuals whose journeys of triumph have shattered barriers, challenged perceptions, and inspired generations. They stand as living testaments to the power of determination, showcasing that neurodiversity is not a hindrance but a wellspring of exceptional abilities. From innovative visionaries to groundbreaking pioneers, these role models exemplify the boundless potential residing within every unique mind.

- **Elon Musk:**

Elon Musk, a renowned entrepreneur, inventor, and visionary behind groundbreaking companies like SpaceX and Tesla, publicly shared his identification with Asperger's syndrome during his appearance on "Saturday Night Live" in May 2021. Musk's openness about his neurodiversity has contributed to raising awareness and fostering acceptance within society.

As the CEO of SpaceX, Musk has significantly impacted space exploration, striving to make space travel more accessible and envisioning human colonization of Mars. His leadership at Tesla, Inc., has revolutionized electric vehicles and renewable energy solutions.

Musk's unique cognitive style, intense focus on his passions, and innovative achievements exemplify how individuals on the autism spectrum can excel and drive innovation in diverse fields. His public acknowledgment of being on the spectrum has inspired many, contributing to a more inclusive understanding of individuals with autism in society.

- **Temple Grandin:**

Dr. Temple Grandin, a renowned professor of animal science, author, and advocate, was diagnosed with autism at a young age. Her work in animal behavior science revolutionized livestock handling and designing humane livestock facilities. Dr. Grandin's advocacy efforts for autism awareness and insightful writings have made her an influential figure, inspiring countless individuals within and outside the autism community.

- **Dan Aykroyd:**

Dan Aykroyd, the beloved actor and comedian known for his roles in movies like "Ghostbusters" and "The Blues Brothers," has openly discussed his experiences with Asperger's syndrome. Despite facing challenges, Aykroyd's successful career in entertainment demonstrates that individuals on the autism spectrum can excel in creative fields, showcasing their unique perspectives and talents.

- **Susan Boyle:**

Susan Boyle, a Scottish singer, gained international fame after her remarkable performance on "Britain's Got Talent." Boyle openly shared her Asperger's diagnosis later in life. Her incredible vocal talent captured the world's attention, showcasing the power of perseverance and unique abilities found in individuals on the autism spectrum.

- **Haley Moss:**

Haley Moss, an attorney, artist, and autism advocate, became the first openly autistic lawyer admitted to the Florida Bar. She has authored books, created art, and uses her platform to advocate for neurodiversity and inclusion. Moss's achievements demonstrate the capabilities of individuals with autism across multiple domains and their potential to drive positive change.

- **Anthony Ianni:**

Anthony Ianni, a former college basketball player, became the first known individual with autism to play Division I college basketball. He's now a motivational speaker advocating for autism awareness, anti-bullying initiatives, and the importance of perseverance in overcoming challenges.

These success stories highlight the remarkable achievements of individuals on the autism spectrum across various fields. Their journeys serve as inspiration, breaking stereotypes and demonstrating that neurodiversity can be a source of unique talents, resilience, and innovation. These role models pave the way for greater acceptance and understanding of neurodiversity in society.

Chapter 11: Resources and Further Assistance

Books, Websites, and Online Communities

Navigating the world of autism spectrum disorder (ASD) involves continuous learning and seeking support from reliable resources. This chapter serves as a guide, presenting an array of valuable sources encompassing books, websites, and online communities designed to empower, educate, and offer a supportive network for individuals, families, educators, and professionals in the autism community.

A. Books:

- **"The Complete Guide to Asperger's Syndrome" by Tony Attwood:** A comprehensive resource providing insights into Asperger's syndrome, exploring characteristics, diagnosis, and strategies for understanding and supporting individuals.
- **"Neurotribes: The Legacy of Autism and the Future of Neurodiversity" by Steve Silberman:** Delving into the history, societal perceptions, and future implications of autism, this book sheds light on the diverse experiences within the autism community.
- **"Uniquely Human: A Different Way of Seeing Autism" by Barry M. Prizant:** Emphasizing the human aspect of autism, this book offers a compassionate perspective, focusing on strengths and promoting understanding and support.
- **"Thinking in Pictures: My Life with Autism" by Temple Grandin:** Temple Grandin's autobiographical work offers a unique insight into her experiences living with autism and how her unique thinking style led to her success.

Websites:

- **Autism Speaks** (www.autismspeaks.org): A comprehensive website providing information on autism research, resources, toolkits for families, and advocacy initiatives.

- **Autism Society** (www.autism-society.org): Offering resources, support groups, and advocacy tools for individuals on the spectrum, their families, and caregivers.
- **The National Autistic Society** (www.autism.org.uk): Providing resources, news, and information about autism services, education, and support for individuals in the UK.
- **Interactive Autism Network (IAN)** (www.iancommunity.org): An online platform for autism research and connecting families with research opportunities and resources.

Online Communities:

- **Reddit - r/autism:** A subreddit dedicated to discussing autism-related topics, sharing experiences, and providing support to individuals and families within the community.
- **Wrong Planet** (www.wrongplanet.net): An online forum and community for individuals on the spectrum to connect, share experiences, and seek advice in a supportive environment.
- **Autistic Self Advocacy Network (ASAN)** (www.autisticadvocacy.org): Focused on advocating for the rights and inclusion of individuals with autism, ASAN provides resources and opportunities for self-advocacy.
- **Facebook Groups - Autism Parent Support Network:** Various Facebook groups exist to offer support and advice to parents and caregivers of individuals with autism, creating a space for sharing experiences and seeking guidance.

These resources serve as a foundation for understanding, guidance, and support within the autism community. Each source aims to empower individuals, families, and professionals with knowledge, connections, and a sense of community, fostering a supportive environment for all involved.

Support Groups and Organizations

Navigating the intricate landscape of autism spectrum disorder (ASD) often necessitates guidance, understanding, and a supportive community. Across the United States, the United Kingdom, and Canada, numerous support groups and organizations have emerged, dedicated to offering resources, advocacy, and a network of support for individuals and families affected by autism.

United States:

- **Autism Society of America:** As one of the oldest autism advocacy organizations in the U.S., the Autism Society provides a broad range of resources, support, and advocacy efforts. Their local chapters offer support groups, educational programs, and initiatives tailored to different regions.
- **Autism Speaks:** A prominent organization that funds research, provides resources, and advocates for policy changes concerning autism. They offer Family Services Grants, resource guides, and toolkits for families and individuals on the spectrum.
- **National Autism Association (NAA):** Focused on supporting families affected by autism, the NAA provides educational resources, safety initiatives, and support programs for caregivers and individuals with autism.

United Kingdom:

- **The National Autistic Society (NAS):** A leading charity organization in the UK, NAS offers a plethora of resources, support services, and advocacy efforts. They provide helplines, online forums, and support groups across the country.
- **Ambitious about Autism:** This charity organization focuses on improving educational opportunities and support for young people with autism. They offer support through their Ambitious College and youth programs.
- **Autism Alliance UK:** A network of autism-focused charities providing various resources, services, and advocacy campaigns across the UK.

They facilitate collaborations and information sharing among member organizations.

Canada:

- **Autism Canada:** A national organization offering resources, education, and advocacy for individuals and families affected by autism. They host webinars, conferences, and offer a range of informative materials.
- **Autism Ontario:** Providing information, support, and advocacy for individuals with autism and their families in Ontario. They offer resources, workshops, and support groups tailored to different regions.
- **Autism Society Canada:** Focused on promoting the understanding, acceptance, and inclusion of individuals with autism. They collaborate with local chapters and organizations to provide support and resources.

These support groups and organizations serve as pillars of strength, offering information, emotional support, and a sense of community to individuals and families navigating the complexities of autism. Their dedication to advocacy, education, and empowerment is instrumental in fostering understanding and improving the lives of those affected by ASD.

Accessing Services and Assistance

Accessing appropriate services and assistance is essential for individuals and families navigating the complexities of autism spectrum disorder (ASD). This chapter aims to provide comprehensive guidance on the process of accessing crucial services, resources, and support systems available for those affected by ASD.

Understanding Available Services:

- **Healthcare Services:** Accessing healthcare services is pivotal. This includes consultations with pediatricians, developmental pediatricians, psychologists, and neurologists specializing in autism assessment and treatment.
- **Educational Services:** Understanding educational rights and accessing

appropriate educational services, such as Individualized Education Programs (IEPs), specialized classrooms, and accommodations, is crucial for the academic success of individuals with ASD.

- **Therapeutic Services:** Accessing various therapies like speech therapy, occupational therapy, applied behavior analysis (ABA), and social skills training can significantly benefit individuals with ASD.

Navigating the Process:

- **Early Intervention Programs:** Exploring early intervention programs that offer services and therapies for infants and toddlers can significantly impact a child's development.
- **Diagnostic and Evaluation Process:** Understanding the diagnostic process, seeking evaluations from professionals specializing in ASD, and obtaining a formal diagnosis is fundamental for accessing appropriate services.
- **Individualized Education Plans (IEPs):** Familiarizing oneself with the process of developing IEPs, attending meetings with educators, and advocating for the specific needs of the individual with ASD is crucial.

Financial Assistance and Support:

- **Government Assistance Programs:** Investigating available government support programs, including Medicaid waivers, Supplemental Security Income (SSI), and tax credits, can aid families in accessing necessary services.
- **Community-Based Resources:** Exploring local support groups, non-profit organizations, and community centers can provide additional resources, emotional support, and guidance.

Advocacy and Seeking Assistance:

- **Advocacy Groups:** Connecting with advocacy groups and organizations specializing in autism can offer guidance, legal advice, and support in accessing services and advocating for rights.

- **Navigating Challenges:** Understanding and overcoming obstacles in accessing services, such as long waiting lists, lack of resources, and bureaucratic processes, requires patience, persistence, and support networks.

Harnessing Technology:

- **Online Resources:** Utilizing online resources, telehealth services, and digital platforms can offer accessible information, support, and connections for families, especially in remote areas.
- **Mobile Applications:** Exploring apps designed for individuals with ASD, offering tools for communication, organization, and skill-building, can supplement traditional services.

Accessing services and assistance for individuals with ASD is a multifaceted journey that requires thorough research, advocacy, and perseverance. Understanding the available services, navigating the system, seeking financial assistance, and leveraging community support networks are crucial steps towards providing comprehensive care and support for individuals and families affected by ASD.

Conclusion

Recap of Key Points

Chapter 1: What is Autism Spectrum Disorder?

- **Defining Autism:** ASD is a spectrum disorder characterized by a wide range of conditions, emphasizing individual differences in behavior and communication.
- **History and Evolution:** Understanding the historical journey and evolving perspectives on autism aids in grasping its complexity.
- **Dispelling Myths:** Addressing misconceptions and myths is essential to fostering a more accurate understanding of ASD.

Chapter 2: Understanding the Autism Spectrum

- **Spectrum Diversity:** Recognizing the diverse nature of ASD and the importance of tailored support based on individual needs.
- **Support Levels:** Understanding varying support requirements and intervention approaches for individuals within the spectrum.
- **Core Characteristics:** Grasping the core characteristics, such as sensory sensitivities and communication challenges, defining ASD.

Chapter 3: Signs and Symptoms of Autism

- **Early Signs:** Identifying early signs in infants and toddlers for early intervention and support.
- **Common Behaviors:** Understanding common behaviors and traits associated with ASD, including social and communication challenges.
- **Co-occurring Conditions:** Recognizing the prevalence of accompanying conditions alongside ASD.

Chapter 4: Diagnosis and Evaluation

- **Diagnostic Process:** Understanding the process and assessments involved in diagnosing ASD.
- **Professionals Involved:** Recognizing the roles of various specialists and professionals in the diagnostic journey.
- **Assessment Criteria:** Familiarizing with assessment criteria and tools used in diagnosing ASD.

Chapter 5: Causes and Risk Factors of Autism

- **Genetic and Environmental Influences:** Grasping the interplay between genetic and environmental factors contributing to ASD.
- **Neurobiology's Role:** Understanding the neurological aspects and brain development linked with ASD.
- **Ongoing Research:** Staying updated with ongoing research and new findings on ASD causes.

Chapter 6: Approaches to Support and Therapy

- **Therapeutic Interventions:** Exploring diverse therapies and treatments available for individuals with ASD.
- **Behavioral Strategies:** Implementing effective strategies for managing behaviors and enhancing communication skills.
- **Alternative Therapies:** Considering complementary approaches to supplement traditional therapies.

Chapter 7: Nurturing Communication and Social Skills

- **Communication Challenges:** Recognizing communication difficulties and implementing enhancements tailored to individual needs.
- **Social Interaction:** Fostering social interaction, building relationships, and addressing challenges in forming connections.
- **Emotional Regulation:** Supporting emotional regulation skills to manage stress and emotional responses.

Chapter 8: Education and Learning Strategies

- **Educational Rights:** Advocating for educational rights, understanding Individualized Education Plans (IEPs), and ensuring accommodations.
- **Classroom Modifications:** Implementing accommodations and modifications in educational settings to support learning.
- **Transitioning to Adulthood:** Exploring post-school options for successful transition to adulthood.

Chapter 9: Supporting Individuals with Autism

- **Family and Community Support:** Recognizing the vital role of family and community in supporting individuals with ASD.
- **Advocacy and Empowerment:** Advocating for rights and empowering individuals with ASD to promote inclusion.
- **Inclusive Environments:** Creating environments that embrace diversity and foster inclusion for individuals with ASD.

Chapter 10: Thriving on the Spectrum: Celebrating Strengths

- **Unique Abilities:** Acknowledging and celebrating the diverse talents and strengths within the autism community.
- **Embracing Neurodiversity:** Promoting acceptance and understanding of neurodiversity, appreciating differences as strengths.
- **Success Stories:** Highlighting inspiring role models and success stories to motivate and inspire others.

Chapter 11: Resources and Further Assistance

- **Informational Resources:** Accessing comprehensive resources, informative websites, and engaging online communities for support.
- **Support Groups and Organizations:** Engaging with support groups dedicated to aiding individuals and families affected by ASD.
- **Accessing Services:** Navigating through services, seeking financial support, and accessing crucial assistance for individuals with ASD.

Encouragement for individuals with autism and their families

Dear friends,

In the tapestry of life, each thread weaves a unique story. For individuals on the autism spectrum and their families, your journey is a testament to resilience, strength, and the beauty of diversity. Your path may have its twists and turns, but within those complexities lie extraordinary stories waiting to unfold.

To those on the spectrum, your uniqueness is not a limitation but a canvas of infinite possibilities. Your way of perceiving the world offers insights and perspectives that enrich our understanding. Embrace your strengths, celebrate your victories, and know that every step you take, every milestone achieved, is a triumph worth cherishing.

To families, your unwavering support, patience, and unconditional love form a bedrock of strength. You are champions in navigating uncharted territories, learning to appreciate the beauty in differences, and fostering an environment where every individual thrives. Your dedication is a guiding light that illuminates the path towards acceptance and understanding.

Remember, each challenge you overcome is a testament to your resilience. Every moment of joy and accomplishment is a testament to your perseverance. You are not alone in this journey; you are part of a community woven together by shared experiences, mutual support, and boundless determination.

In times of uncertainty, hold onto hope. Seek solace in the power of togetherness, find strength in your unique abilities, and draw inspiration from the many success stories that pave the way. Your journey is one of courage, compassion, and immeasurable worth.

May you find comfort in the knowledge that your presence enriches our world, and your journey, though filled with challenges, is also brimming with endless possibilities. Embrace your journey, celebrate your uniqueness, and continue to shine brightly, for your light illuminates the way for a more inclusive and compassionate world.

With heartfelt encouragement,
Mandhouj Nadiya

Don't miss out!

Visit the website below and you can sign up to receive emails whenever Nedia Mandhouj publishes a new book. There's no charge and no obligation.

https://books2read.com/r/B-A-VIUBB-VRLRC

Also by Nedia Mandhouj

Understanding and Celebrating Autism : A Beginner's Comprehensive Guide